Forex:

Do's And Don'ts To Make Money Online Trading

2nd Edition

Table of Contents

Introduction

Trade has been a part and parcel of our lives since time immemorial. First there was the barter system and then came the system to exchange goods for gold coins.

Most trade that occurred at the time was internal trade, as the transport system was not well developed. But with time, that too saw a drastic improvement and people bought and sold every day goods overseas.

Right from the biblical era, foreign exchange has been carried out to in order to improve the relationships with the traders of foreign countries and also boost local business.

Initially, the traders would agree on gold coins and exchange the agreed value. But with time, they realized that gold was a scarce commodity and could not really be used to deal in everyday trade. That is when *currency* was invented.

Traders began to implement the system of paying with their local currency. But that started to pose a challenge to these traders as each country started having their own currency. They had to make use of foreign currency to buy goods from a foreign land, which was tough to attain. The traders would often engage in fights and not know how to go about trading.

With time, the system evolved and the traders opened up bank accounts in the foreign countries. They would buy the local currency and store it at these banks, which would make it extremely easy for them to trade with foreign traders.

Slowly, the trend intensified and started gaining momentum. During the early 1900's traders realized that it was possible for them to capitalize on the rate differences amongst the currencies.

Currency exchange then gained popularity and the traders started selling their local currency to acquire foreign currency. Special banks were then set up to deal in this trade alone and gave traders an opportunity to indulge in exchange with ease.

During the dotcom bubble that occurred in the later 90's and early 2000's, regular people started trading in foreign currencies. They would login to their online accounts and buy and sell currencies. That is how the current foreign exchange system came into being.

Now better known as *Forex*: foreign exchange refers to buying and selling currencies in order to realize a profit. Through the course of this book, we will look at how you can trade in forex and the different concepts that you should acquaint yourself with in order to carry out this type of trade.

I thank you for choosing this book and hope you have a good time reading it.

Chapter 1: What is forex Trading? The Different Concepts Explained

Forex is a trading term that is used to describe foreign exchange. This foreign exchange is the exchange of currencies. The trader uses his currency to buy a currency pair that will help him realize a profit.

Foreign exchange gained popularity in the last decade or so owing to the changes that took place in the economic market. Certain countries' currencies increased greatly in value, which made them lucrative investment choices. It suddenly became easier for the common man to buy and sell foreign currencies thereby further boosting its trade.

Let us now look at an example to understand forex trade better.

Now say for example you are living in the US and wish to buy cheese from France. When you pay the local dealer in France, he will obviously only accept Euro and not the dollar. So, you will have to exchange your dollar for euro. Here, you cannot give 1 dollar and get 1 euro in return. There will be a difference in the currency rates where one will always trail and the other one will be valued higher.

The difference in the rate will be determined by many factors, which we will discuss later in this book.

So, say the value of 100 dollar equals 92 euros. By exchanging your dollars, you are reducing the value of the currency, as you will only be getting 92 euros in return. These are just imaginary figures and meant to show you how the forex markets operate. The real figures will be much different. The euro might trail the dollar sometimes owing to the economic conditions.

In this example we looked at two currencies that are quite close to each other in value. But there are some currencies that will lie on the extreme end of the spectrum. Take for example the Indian rupee. 1 American dollar is valued at 65 Indian rupee or INR. This means that the American trader can increase his money's value 65 times by opting to exchange the dollar for the rupee.

Similarly, you have to find two currency pairs that will allow you to remain with a big profit when you exchange them. There are many currencies in the world and you have to acquaint yourself with each and each of their values if you wish to trade in Forex.

Let us now focus on some of their basic concepts.

Trading type

Most of the foreign currencies are traded over the counter. This means that they are not listed on any of the different stock exchanges. There are many traders in the market that will know where to buy these foreign currencies. You have to contact any of these and they will get you the desired money. But you have to be well aware of the trending rates in the market in order to buy and sell them at the right price.

The important currencies

 There are a few important currencies that are traded on a regular basis in the forex market. These are important mainly because they belong to countries that are doing very well economically. Their economic stability makes them great choices, especially if you are looking for currencies that are dependable. These are better known as the major eight as they belong to eight countries that are doing very well for themselves. Let us look at these eight countries and their respective currencies. The US dollar, Canadian dollar, United Kingdom pound sterling, Switzerland euro, Australian dollar, New Zealand dollar and the Japanese yen, all of these are traded on a regular basis and are great investment choices to make. You can avail stability by investing in these and not have to worry about too many fluctuations. Remember that these should be considered as your strong currencies that will then be paired with a weak one to arrive at a profit.

The worldwide currency market is one of the largest and most complicated in the world. Trillions of dollars routinely flow through it, contributed by individuals like you as well as hedge funds, corporations and banks. When it comes to forex trading, more than 75 percent of all the trading that happens is speculative in nature. This speculation is driven by a number of factors which will be discussed in detail below.

When it comes to currency exchange rates, the most critical factor to consider is the yield. The major eight all have national banks that determine their interest rates which means that even a small variation in these numbers can affect the currency in a major way. This occurs as a result of speculators like you buying high yield currencies and selling those with a low yield. For example, in 2006 there was a point where the United States had an interest rate of 5.25 percent in the short term while that same period of time in Japan yielded a .25 percent interest rate. This allowed those who took advantage of it to gain a substantial return while at the same time profiting for appreciation as well.

Exchange rates can also be affected by economic growth, also known as their gross domestic product or simply, GDP. The growth or decline of the economy of one of the major eight will in turn affect their interest rates either raising them as the GDP expands or lowering them as it contracts. This leads to large speculative swings when the GDP makes a large move that is not echoed in interest rates in a reasonable fashion. It is important to be aware of these movements but not overly eager to act on them without additional information.

Behind interest rates and economic growth, politics in the major eight can lead to major swings in how that currency trades as speculative traders are always more likely to jump ship at the sign of a geopolitical dustup, long before any results have been determined. These types of situations will routinely trump the actual economics at play on a given day and as such should be watched closely.

For example, in the middle of 2005 the United States dollar was quite strong compared to the Canadian dollar despite the fact that Canada was providing more crude oil to the United States than anyone else in the world. This occurred because then Canadian Prime Minister Paul Martin had gotten himself into a situation where he was being accused of corruption. This political scandal trumped the truth of the situation for weeks and it was only after it had blown over that the position between the two dollars stabilized.

It is also important to monitor capital flows compared to trade flows behind those discussed above. Trade flow can be considered any income a country makes from trade and capital flow can be measured by noting how interested foreign powers are investing in the country. This can be difficult however as some of the major eight react more to trade flow while others react more to capitol flow. A good rule of thumb is that the currency markets of New Zealand, Australia, Japan, Germany and Canada are more likely to be influenced by trade flows, the rest are more likely to respond to trade flow influxes.

The most relevant example of this idea is the current position the United States finds itself in. While the United States has historically held an extremely large deficit this fact is offset in the currency market due to the fact that it also has a large amount of capital flow to balance everything out. If this were to change however the market would then fluctuate wildly which is why it pays to monitor capital and trade flow closely.

Finally, acquisitions and mergers are also known to influence currency prices, though it is less common for them to do so compared with the factors discussed above. This only occurs when a substantial corporation from one of the major eight makes a move to acquire a substantial corporation of another. These situations can have a wide variety of effects on the currency market depending on the corporations in question. It is important to stay up to date on business news just in case.

Buying and selling

There are many concepts in forex that you have to thoroughly understand if you wish to realize a big profit from it. One such concept is that of buying and selling. Buying and selling refers to you buying a currency by pledging another. So, if you are buying American dollars then you will be pledging Chinese yuan against it. You have to go through a certain process where first you will exchange your local money to attain the dollars and then exchange that for the yuan. This process will seem a little complicated but is actually quite simple. You don't really have to be an expert in the field and can carry out the trade quite easily, provided you go about it in the prescribed manner.

Returns

The returns that your forex trade will provide you are quite noteworthy. Forex has the capacity to provide you with the power to control as much as $100,000 just by investing $100 towards it. That is how lucrative your forex business can be. But for that, you have to know how to use the different currency pairs to your advantage. There are stories of how people have turned their marginal profits into extreme profits just by choosing to deal in foreign currencies. You too can scale such heights by taking it up, but you have to also prepare for the other side of the coin. Forex has the power to turn your profits into losses. You might end up losing out on a lot of money owing to making the wrong investments or being in a hurry to dispose of what you are holding. The forex markets can be a bit unpredictable and if you end up choosing the wrong currency pairs then you will lose out on your investment money. So the bottom line is to prepare for roaring success as also unpredictable losses.

Two times benefits

With foreign currency investments you can avail dual benefits. This means that you can capitalize on a currency's steady nature and derive a profit from it. Say for example you exchanged 200 yen for a dollar bond that will pay you 10% provided the value of the currency remains stable. This is a great opportunity for you to capitalize on the scheme as you can wait out a period of time and hope that the difference remains the same. Say after 2 years, your bond has matured; you can exchange it for the new value and also avail the cess provided the rates have remained the same. This is a good thing, as the rates will not drastically vary over the years. So just with the one investment you have the choice to ring in dual benefits.

These form the different concepts of forex trading that you have to acquaint yourself with in order to start trading.

Trader types defined

There is an art or skill into doing something to gain maximum profits or to excel. The same goes for forex Trading. In forex trading, you need to listen to your guts and your instincts; you also need to have some depth in trading knowledge, intelligence as well striking at the right time. Timing is definitely a huge influence in the foreign exchange world and this is also something novice traders ignore.

Different traders have different trade secrets and their own personal formula for success. Below are a few examples of trader behavior and the psychology of timing that can be used to your advantage.

a) *The Day Trader- The day trader, obviously, trades for the day. These traders by practice will not hold anything after a trading session closes and their trading style is always trades in high-volume. A short-term trader's typical day generally involves a quick turnover rate on one or more trades and this can range between 10- to 100-times the normal transaction volume. The idea is to reap in more earnings from a small swing. Traders who work in this style will use shorter time-frame charts either in one-, five- or 15-minute periods. Day traders also rely more on technical trading patterns and volatile pairs in order to attain profits. The currency pair of GBP/JPN is one such example of volatile pairs and it is great for short term traders because its average hourly pips range can go up to 100 pips.*

b) *Swing Trader- The swing trader has major advantage of time, where he takes in a longer time frame to trade and will sometimes hold positions from a mere couple of hours to even days or weeks. This is all done in the hopes to call a turn in the market. The swing trader looks to make earnings from an entry into the market unlike the day trader. Timing is imperative for the swing trader because of this entry element. Swing traders are more likely to prefer a more liquid currency pair such as the GBP/USD.*

c) *The Position Trader- The position trader's method is different from the day or swing trader mainly due to her perspective of the market. They don't monitor short term market movements because their eyes are fixed on the long term plan. The Position Trader can have a strategy that can go on for hours, days, weeks and sometimes months and years. Position traders are more likely to look at longer term fundamental models and opportunities.* They will analyze and compare economic models, governmental decisions as well as interest rates when making their trading decisions.

News Releases

Whether you are a trader day, swing or position- all traders will look at news releases because this may affect the market. No matter whether they central bank press releases, economic announcements, business announcements or even governmental decisions, all traders would need to make adjustments to their trading decisions following a news release.

The right time to trade

Forex Trading is different from other markets because of its capability to trade for twenty four hours every day, throughout the week. But each trading day consists of multiple trading sessions which are famously known as the Asian session, American session and European session. These sessions are known as the Tokyo, New York and London sessions respectively. Different countries operate at different times because there is no single exchange in the forex market. When traders have ceased trading operations for the day in Sydney, the forex traders in New York are beginning their trading day.

Each trading sessions has their own unique characteristics so there really isn't any right or wrong to a trading time, but knowing what a good time and bad time is can take you from a novice trader to an expert in no time.

Each trading session in the world is driven by its economies that are active therefore each session has its own unique characteristic. There are no open sessions during the weekend. On a 7 day week, trading essentially begins when Sydney/Tokyo starts trading at the beginning of the week, and it finishes when New York closes its sessions at the end of the week. The opening and closing sessions also depend on where you are located in the world. For Japan, the trading week starts on Monday whereas in London, the trading week begins on Sunday evening.

The Asian Session

The Asian session begins at 22.00 GMT, which is when Sydney opens. Trading volumes are comparatively small because only Sydney is trading at this time. Price changes are expected to be minimal compared to other sessions.

At approximately 00.00 GMT, Tokyo opens its doors and subsequently increases trading volume. Nevertheless, price changes at this point is still considered small to moderate since Australia & Japan are relatively small markets compared to that of Europe and USA. The spreads on major currency pairs are likely to be higher during these times but the liquidity will not be as high as they are in Europe & US.

At the Asian session, the Japanese Yen, Australian Dollar and New Zealand Dollar are the frequently traded currencies because these are the currencies used at the market that opens at the Asian session. Currency pairs that are often traded are AUD/USD, AUD/JPY, AUD/NZD, JPY/USD, NZD/JPY and NZD/USD.

The European Session

The London Session opens approximately at 8.00 GMT and that is the last hour of trading in Tokyo. Despite that, half of the world is awake at this time and that means a higher number of investors would also be trading in the market. Large movements happen in the market compared to the Asian session. Day traders transition from exciting the Asian market and entering positions in Europe.

At the European session, all currency pairs are traded because there is no significant difference in currency exchange behavior. Spreads are smaller because there is a much higher volume in this session and thus, more liquidity. The London session observes more liquidity than any other session because its market accounts for almost 38% of the total market volume. New York commands 17% whereas Japan is 6%.

The American session

The New York Session opens at the same time with the London session, at 13.00 GMT. Volume and volatility is increased because of the combined participants from both these sessions. At 17.00 GMT, the London session closes while the New York session is in trade by itself, until the Asians starts trading again.

During this time, there is a decrease in trading volume since the European traders are done for the day. At the New York session, all currency pairs are traded.

Why is the forex market preferred?

There are many reasons that make the forex market a very desirable place to invest in. here are some of the reasons for the same.

Liquidity

The first and most important reason why the forex market is the most preferred market is because of the liquidity of the currencies. You don't have to put in too much effort to dispose off your currencies. There will be a ready audience for it willing to buy it from you. You don't have to wait for some time like you would in the stock market to dispose off your shares. You can give the sell command and your currencies will be sold.

24 hours trading

The forex market is open 24 hours a day, 3965 days a year. This means that there are no trading hours like you have with your stock markets. You can buy and sell currencies any time that you like and don't have to wait for the right time. Since these currencies are all bought and sold around the world, you might have to time your trade with the foreign country's morning hours if you wish to indulge in smooth sailing trading. You won't have to panic about getting into a deal before the closing bell and can invest leisurely.

Transaction costs

The transaction costs are very low in the forex market. There are no middle men who will add to your costs and so, you will not have to shell out a large sum to pay for your forex transactions. You will only have to take care of the fees that your broker or the trading company might charge you.

Bull market

The forex market is known as a perpetually bull market. This means that at no time will all the currency rates drop and you can choose two extreme currencies and pit them against each other to realize a big profit.

No governing body

There is no governing body for the forex market and trade is free conducted in the different economic markets. These governing bodies can sometimes create a ruckus with their rules and restrictions that can hamper trade. But that problem is effectively dealt with in the forex market.

These form the different reasons that make the forex market an ideal place to invest money in.

Chapter 2: Getting Started with forex

In the previous chapter; we looked at the meaning and different concepts of forex trading and in this one, we will look at how you can get started with Forex.

As you know, there are some basic and some specific things that you must ready in order to trade in forex exchange and they are explained as under.

Basics

Laptop

The first and most basic thing that you will require to trade in forex is a laptop. You have to buy one and use it only for trading purposes. You don't really have to buy a fancy high quality one and can choose one that will serve the purpose. You have to place it in a dedicated room in order to take it up seriously. It is also a good idea to set up a desktop system, as that will prevent you from carrying the computer around and losing your interest in the trade.

Internet

The next thing is a reliable internet connection. As you know, the internet is the most important aspect of trading. You need the internet to look at the rates and also buy and sell the currencies. If you live in an area where the internet is shaky then you should invest in a dongle that will help you remain connected even if the internet stops working. Remember that the forex market can be just as volatile as your regular stock market and it is important that you remain prepared to take quick actions, which is only possible if you have a strong internet connection.

Trading account/ online account

The next step is to open a trading account. The trading account should be specific to forex trading. You can call up the company that deals with it and ask them to help you open the account. Most companies today send their representative over to your place to help you get started with an account. You can also start an online account, as that will make it easy for you to trade by yourself without having to rely on a broker.

Software

There might be some software that the company officials will download onto your system. You have to allow them to do that, as that is what will help you trade in Forex. The software is generally generic and will not take any more than an hour to download. Once it has been installed, you have to ask the installer to help you understand the software and how you can use it. If you are not accustomed to it at all then you should take notes and clear everything out before going about using it. Remember that you will be yourself be buying and selling the currencies so you will have to acquaint yourself with using the software.

Specifics

Forex broker

The first specific thing to find yourself is a forex broker. A broker is who will help you buy and sell the foreign currencies. The broker has to be forex specific if you wish to make the most of your investments. Try to find a part time broker if you are willing to do most of the research. If you have no time to conduct the research and will prefer to have someone do it for you then you can choose a full time broker. The broker should be reliable and the two of you should be on the same page at all times.

When you are researching various brokers and brokerages it is important to consider a number of factors to ensure you are placing your trust in the right place. First of all, it is important to ensure that the brokerage you ultimately choose is one that has been in business for at least 10 years. This ensures your choice has the experience to handle clients properly. Newer flash-in-the-pan brokerages might try and entice you with a wide variety of "good bargains" don't be fooled, experience trumps a good sales pitch in the long run every time.

The next thing to consider when choosing a brokerage is to ensure that it voluntarily submits to a major government oversight committee. Submitting to oversight ensures that your broker is transparent and honest in every one of their dealings. In the United States there are two groups that oversee brokerages, the Commodity Futures Trading Commission and the National Futures Association.

From there it is important to determine how many types of trading the brokerage specializes in. Larger brokerages typically have better success rates due to their enhanced grasp of the markets as a whole. On the other hand, dedicated brokerages can have a detailed grasp of specifics that a larger brokerage might miss. As such it is important to read plenty of client reviews across a multitude of sites to get a feel for each brokerage's results. It is important to take each review you read with a grain of salt as it could easily be skewed in one direction or another. Instead, use the reviews to get an overall feel for the brokerage.

Finally, it is important to ensure that whatever brokerage you do end up going with has a few essentials that are non-negotiable. It is important that they have a modern looking, professional website. A dated or other faulty website is a sign that something there is not quite right, steer clear of that brokerage or you will regret it later. Likewise, it is important that the rates they charge for each trade transaction meet the current standards. A reasonable rate is 4 cents per side and 8 cents per round turn on micro lots, 40 cents per side and 80 cents per round turn on mini lots and 4 dollars per side and 8 dollars per round turn for standard lots.

Information

The next step is to gather specific information about forex trade. Foreign exchange is a subject that requires you to conduct some research and only then will you be able to conduct it on a daily basis. The information can be acquired through this book alone. But you can also turn to other sources to seek your information. As long as you remain prepared for the trade with the right information you are good to start with forex trading.

Forex journal

The forex market is quite volatile. You have to understand how it works and also pay attention to all your trades. In order to arrive at a winning strategy you have to maintain a record of all your deals. For that, you should maintain a journal and write down all your trades. You must also record all your mistakes in order to refer back at them and not repeat them again. The journal can be an online journal or a physical journal. The former will help you access it at any time and any place and the latter will give you a personal feel.

Currency choice

The next step is to pick the currency. The currency should be chosen in pairs. As you saw in the previous chapter, the currencies that you pick need to be picked in pairs. It is best to pick an extreme pair like a currency that is doing extremely well and one that is doing poorly.

These form the different things that you must prepare in order to carry out the day-to-day trades. You have to pick the best of each, as your business quality will depend on it. Do not compromise on any of these steps.

Examples of forex Trading

Going Long on GBP/USD (Sterling/US dollar)

In this example, we are looking at a fixed spread on GBD/USD at a 2 pip spread.

The Scenario:

It is the first Friday of the month and we are going to assume that the GBP/USD is currently trading at 1.5686/1.5688. The concern at the moment is the employment situation in the US, and this is affecting trader's sentiments.

As a trader, you expect that the USD will weaken and the GBP will strengthen against the USD and you go ahead to buy (go long) £20,000 on GBP/USD at 1.5688.

The trade size is in units of the base currency in the pair. You choose a leverage scale of 60:1 for this trade and it requires a deposit of (£20,000*1.5688/50) $627.52.

True to your anticipation, the pound does strengthen against the dollar and when it hits 1.5750, you decide to cash in your profits. Right now, the new price is 1.5750/1.5752 and you sell to close at 1.5750.

The Results: You bought at 1.5688 and sold at 1.5750, a rise of 62 pips.

Your Profit: (1.5750 – 1.5688) x 10,000 = $62.

Going Short on EUR/USD (Euro/US dollar)

In this example, we are trading the EUR/USD at 1.3360/1.3361.

The Scenario:

It is mid-July and investors are worried about the sovereign debt crisis and its impact on the US economy. You as a trader, expect the Euro to fall against the USD. So you decide to sell (go short) €10,000 on EUR/USD at 1.3360.

Your choice of leverage is 20:1 for this trade and this requires a deposit of (€10,000*1.3360/20) $668.00.

So you got it right! The Euro depreciated against the USD to 1.3251 and you decide to close your trade and take your profits. The new price is now at 1.3250/1.3251 and you buy to close at 1.3251.

The Result: You sold at 1.3360 and bought at 1.3251, a fall of 109 pips,

Your Profit: You just raked in a profit of (1.3360 - 1.3251) x 10,000 = $109.

Going long on USD/JPY (US dollar/Japanese yen)

For this example, the USD/JPY is trading at 96.39/96.40.

It is mid-March and the Japanese yen has surged and is recovering from the worst earthquake in the country's history. There is high demand for the yen as international businesses are vying to come in to redevelop the devastated areas.

The Scenario

You expect that the yen will fall back against the US dollar as it is too strong now. So you go long and buy $10,000 on USD/JPY at 96.40.

Your leverage scale is 25:1 with an initial deposit of ($10,000*96.40/25) 38,560 yen.

The Result: Unfortunately, your prediction went wrong and the dollar continued its descent against the Yen, falling to a record low of 95.25. You just lost (96.40 − 95.25) x 10,000 = 11500 yen.

Going short on USD/CAD (US dollar/Canadian dollar)

For this example, the USD/CAD is trading at 1.0320/1.0324.

The Scenario

It is mid-summer and the US currency is being weighed down by lack of progress to raise the US debt ceiling.

So, you think that the USD/CAD will decline even more so you go short $10,000 on USD/CAD at 1.0320

The Result: Your expectations prove right! The US dollar reaches to an all time low of 1.0234 against the Canadian dollar. So you take your profits at this point. The new price is 1.0230/1.0234 and you can therefore buy to close at 1.0234.

Your Profit: You sold at 1.0320 and bought at 1.0234, a drop of 86 pips. This gives you a profit of: (1.0320 − 1.0234) x 10,000 = CAD86.

Chapter 3: Companies That Provide forex Services

Now that you looked at how you can get started with forex trading we can now look at the different companies that help you trade in these currencies.

Banks

Banks are the first and primary source of Forex. They have direct access to the different banks located in foreign countries and can easily avail the currencies. Whenever you buy or sell currencies, a certain interest fee will be attached to it. These banks will only attach a nominal value that is quite reasonable. You will have to first open an account with the bank and then add in money into the account. The bank will then use the same money to buy the currencies for you. You have to tell them how much you wish to convert.

The most preferred banks and their forex market shares are mentioned as under.

Citibank, -16.04%, Deutsche bank-15.67%, Barclay's investment bank-10.91%, UBS AG-10.88% and HSBC-7.12%.

You can choose any one of these to be your forex banker. You have to check the rate of commission that they charge.

Forex companies

It is understood that banks are the leading institutions that help in dealing with Forex. But apart from banks there are also certain companies that will help you out. These are known as forex companies and are licensed to carry out the different trades. They will also charge a certain commission for their trade, which might be slightly higher than what your banks will charge you.

Here is a list of the best forex companies that you can approach Hot Forex, XE Markets, Delta stock Ad, Tele trade DJ Ltd. and Xness Group.

These are present all over the world and you have to open an account with each in order to trade with them.

Traveler exchanges

Apart from these two, you can also buy foreign currencies from traveler exchanges. Sometimes, these will provide you with a good exchange rate, which will be pocket friendly. But you have to choose something that is reliable and has a good reputation. You can look up these exchanges online and visit them. They will mostly be present in small markets where tourists frequently visit.

There are some reputed companies like western union and American express that you can approach to have your money exchanged.

Chapter 4: forex Fundamental and Technical Analysis

In the forex market, you have to conduct three main types of research in order to invest in the right place. These form the fundamental, technical and sentimental analysis. All three are extremely important and you have to understand each in order to carry them out. Let us look at each of them in detail.

Fundamental analysis

The fundamental analysis is a type of analysis that you conduct to understand the country's economic condition and how it will impact the value of the currency. Fundamental analysis is generally conducted in the stock market to understand whether the company is a good one or not. But there is a lot of difference between the two, and you cannot use the same tools to surmise the two types of fundamental analysis. Let us look at the different things that you should consider to understand the fundamentals of an economic market.

Prevailing interest rates

The interest rates that prevail in the country will determine the value of the currency. These interest rates are what the local bank charges for the loans and gives away for the deposits. There has to be a difference between the two rates and only then will there be stability. That is determined by the specific country's central bank. When a person avails a loan he will end up making the bank richer and thereby contribute to the country's economy. You have to look into the interest rates and also be aware of any changes that might occur in it. The central bank can at any time change the rate of interest, which will have a direct impact on the currency value.

Employment statistics

The employment statistics of the country will also have a direct bearing on the value of the currency. Employment contributes to the economy in two ways. First, it will give people buying power, as more salaries will be doled out to the crowd. The other way is that people will buy the different goods and services thereby contributing to the growth of the economy. So, you have to look at how many people are employed in the country and also check the number of unemployed. Third world countries will have very little people employed, which means that the value of their currency will be very weak. The opposite applies to developed countries.

Gross domestic product

Gross domestic product refers to the per capita income and the overall money that the country collectively earns. You have to look at the GDP of a country to see if its currency will do well or not. There is divided opinion on how the GDP of a country has to be assessed. Some are of the opinion that a rise in the GDP is a good sign as it signifies economic stability. On the other hand, some look at it as a bad thing as it will cause the consumer goods prices to rise, which will again impact the currency value negatively.

Commodity prices

The commodity prices of a country will also determine the value of the currency. As you know, people have to buy and sell these goods and if it is too high then the buying capacity will reduce, that will in turn cause the value to drop. That is not a good sign. You have to look for a country where the prices are nominal and it is possible for a majority to afford the goods and services.

Political causes

There are certain political causes that can affect the value of the currency. If there is an election or if there is protest then it will have an impact on the value of the currency. You have to watch the news regularly to be acquainted with any such changes and prepare for it. If you think a political uproar is going to cause the value of the currency drop then you have to dispose it off at the earliest.

Natural causes

There are certain natural calamities that can impact the value of the currency. These can include earthquakes, tsunamis etc. You have to read the newspaper regularly to know of these and remain prepared for any price changes.

These form the different things that you have to bear in mind while performing fundamental analysis.

With all of these factors contributing to variations in currency market price, it is easy to see that any type of commentary, political or economic news from a reliable source that runs counter to current trends the market is experiencing at the moment can cause dramatic variations in price. It is important to understand that these changes do not occur immediately however, the currency market is too large and varied for that. Instead, for you that means forewarned is forearmed and that the longer you know about an event before the wider world is the more you can profit from the information gap. This can take as long as several days depending on the factors involved and should not be discounted under any circumstances.

Technical analysis

Technical analysis is a type of statistical analysis that you use to understand the technical aspect of the trade. You will be able to statistically predict the rise and fall in the rates of the currencies. Here are the different things that you have to calculate for it.

Moving averages

The very first thing that you have to calculate is the moving averages. Moving averages are of three types - the simple, the weighted and the exponential moving averages. All three require you to indulge in some calculations that are meant to help you understand how the rates of the currencies will move. If you are not good at math then you can avail the help of a friend to perform the different calculations. This is the most sought after and trusted form of prediction techniques used in the world of Forex.

Fibonacci numbers

Those of you that know about the Fibonacci series will be able to use this technique. The Fibonacci series follows a set pattern of values and so will the currency rates. You have to understand how to apply it to the currency rates and use it to your advantage. Again, you can avail the help of a friend or a family member to help calculate the trend values.

Bollinger bands

Bollinger bands are the next statistical tool that you can use to calculate the changes in the trends. For this, you have to understand and identify a certain pattern that the currency is following. Based on it, you will be able to predict the future of the currency. Bollinger bands are an extremely popular way of helping speculators determine whether a trend actually exists or if its indicating factors were more of a fluke. They are especially usefully when determining when a certain currency reaches a point of oversaturation.

Stochastic oscillator

The stochastic oscillator is a type of technical tool that will help you conduct an in depth research into the manner in which the different currency prices will vary. This technique can be a little complex but there are many software that you can make use of to calculate this with ease.

RSI

The RSI stands for relative strength index. It is one that will provide you with a scale to measure your currency's worth. After you apply the strategy and arrive at a number, you can proceed to the next step. The next step involves looking at the value of the number and seeing if it is less than 30. If it is, then it means that the currency is undervalued. If it is over 70 then it means that the currency is overbought.

As a rule, currencies are more likely to experience influence from longer, more persistent trends than those in other markets. A good analogy to consider is that currencies are like transcontinental ships at sea, they may vary a little but their routes tend to be well defined. The trick then becomes knowing the right predefined routes to trust. This is where technical analysis comes in as it will allow you to find the trends where they are hiding among the random multitude of variables that might be affecting them in one way or another.

Candlesticks

This form of technical analysis works by looking for certain patterns among the open and close as well as the low and high for a specific security over a variable amount of time. When these data points present a noticeable pattern it allows speculators to sell or buy currencies based on assumptions that can be made about each pattern.

A candlestick can be broken down into two parts, a vertical line which shows the range of trading that happened in a given period and a bar connected to the vertical line which shows the ultimate difference between where the currency started a day and where it ended. The wide part is referred to as the real body, if the real body is colored in then you can assume the difference for the day was negative while a real body that is just an outline indicates a positive difference for the day.

The vertical line is then referred to as the shadow of the real body. If the shadow above the candle is short while the real body is colored in, then the starting price of the day was near the high for the day. If the shadow is short on a day where the real body is just an outline, then the price at the close of the market was near the high for the day.

In what is known as the morning start formation you take a look at three days' worth of candlesticks for a single currency. The first candle in this formation should be definitely negative and indicate guaranteed losses. The second should begin near the end of the first candle, be contained in a narrow range and contain a high that is above the middle of the initial candle. The final candle should be completely positive with a close above the middle of the initial candle. This formation will indicate a strong reversal in a longstanding downward trend. This means that the price should not fall below document lows and is likely to see a reversal of fortune soon.

The evening star formation is more or less the opposite of the morning star. The initial candle will be extremely positive with the second staying almost completely above it. The final candle will then be startlingly negative with a close that is below the middle of the initial candle. From this you can infer that the currency has hit a ceiling and that additional downward slopes are likely.

A hammer formation occurs when the real body of the candle sits atop a very long shadow. This indicates that the price of the currency changed dramatically throughout the day but the end result is nearly the same. This indicates a bullish market which overcame what was originally a bearish start. The shooting star formation is the opposite of the hammer and finds the real body at the bottom of a long shadow. Nevertheless, this is an indicator of potential increased growth in the future.

Making trades in forex markets using candlestick formations can provide you with additional reference points when looking to understand trend lines or Fibonacci potential. Using candlestick patterns also makes it easy to quickly grasp a wide variety of disparate information. It is best used with firm stop loss orders set to determine if the market follows the suggested pattern. Failing to implement stop loss orders can easily lead to major losses when markets don't react as expected.

Sentimental analysis

Sentimental analysis refers to understanding the mood of the investors and the market as a whole. You have to understand both thoroughly if you wish to make the most of your forex investments. As you know, the theory of demand and supply greatly affects the prices of currencies. You have to assess this by knowing whether the market is interested in investing in a certain stock or not. That is only possible if you study the market trends and read the news regularly.

While picking successful trends using sentimental analysis can be difficult, using the sentimental analysis of others is an easy way to make beneficial trades. If you keep up on the specifics it can be easier to note when one part of the market is responding to sentimental analysis which is when you wait for that to backfire and reap the rewards after things have stabilized.

These form the different types of analysis that you have to conduct in order to make the right forex investment choices.

Chapter 5: forex Winning Strategies

Trading in forex might seem like a daunting task but really isn't. You have to make use of certain tips and tricks that will help you realize a big profit. Let us look at them in detail in this chapter.

Demand and supply imbalance

The very first strategy is to spot a supply and demand imbalance. It is obvious that you have to capitalize on such a situation if you wish to avail a definite profit. This has nothing to do with the buy low sell high theory. Here, you have to look for currency pairs that are in high demand and it is probably going go higher. You must also see that there are very little sellers. You have to bid for such a pair and wait patiently. As soon as you are awarded the currency you have to hold on to it until such time as the value goes up and the demand is still high. You will be able to sell it off with ease and ring in a profit. You have to scour for such currencies and bid for them early in order to get them.

Gettable Targets

Remember to set gettable targets with your trades. This is a big secret that many people overlook when they begin trading in the forex market. You have to set targets that are easily attainable. If you aim too high then you will wait on it for too long. Don't be greedy, pick something that you will be able to attain fast and chase it. But at the same time, you should not set something that too low. Try to aim at least for the stars to get to the top of the tree.

Risk-reward ratio

When you are setting the risk and reward ratio, it should be 3:1. This means that you should calculate for 3 times the risk than the reward if you wish to remain with a big profit. Think of it as a way to safeguard your investment. You have to decide on the numbers in advance. Say for example you are investing $500 to acquire a currency pair. You have to then calculate the risk on it. Say you decide on a risk of 30%, which means that you are expecting to lose around $150. You have to set a profit margin of 10%, so, you have to expect $50 from the deal. Doing so will help you remain on the right track.

Range trading

You have to indulge in range trading. This is a winning strategy that many successful investors indulge in. They will pick a particular range and trade within the same. It provides them a certain sense of security and also the freedom to make their decision. Pick the range on a daily basis instead of choosing it in advance. The range should be based on the highest and the lowest that the currency might touch.

Price action

Price action is another technique that you can implement. It refers to one where you determine which currency to invest in based on its momentum. Now let us say a currency value is falling, you have to assume that it will keep falling and not invest in it. On the other hand, if a particular currency's value is on the rise then you have to assume that it will keep rising. You have to invest in it immediately in order to capitalize on the situation.

Trend following

The next strategy is to follow a trend. The trend here refers to the prevailing market trend. You have to look at certain currencies that are in demand and buy them in order to make a profit. You have to base your judgment on the fact that it is always a safe bet to stay with the herd instead of wandering off, as chances of you getting lost are high. So, it is best for you to do as the rest of the crowd does. You have to look at news forecasts to pick the best currency pairs.

Contrarian trading

Contrarian trading is the opposite of the above-mentioned strategy. It is one where you do not follow the crowd and go against it. The idea here is to do things differently and exploit the situation. So if everybody is interested in a certain currency then you should go against it and sell any that you have in your possession. If everyone is selling a certain currency, then you should quickly buy them. This is the type of thinking that helps many investors ring in huge profits.

Arbitrage Trading

Arbitrage trading is a type of trading that can be pointed to the acquisition and loss of billions upon billions of dollars annually. At its most basic, arbitrage can be seen as the art of finding points in the currency market where one currency is undervalued while another is overvalued and finding the right set of trades in order to force the under/overvaluation to result in a profit. This may sound similar to value trading but the crucial difference here is that with a value trade you hope to make a profit, with an arbitrage trade you know you will make a profit.

For example, if you assume that GBP/USD, EUR/GDP and USD/EUR pairs are listed at 1.6388, .7231 and 1.1837 then if you purchase a single mini amount of EUR you could then sell most of it for just over £7,000 and then sell that for just shy of $12,000 which means you will have made a total of $13 on each trade without any risk as all of your positions cancel each other out across each currency.

What is extremely important for those who practice forex arbitrage to understand is that exploiting an arbitrage scenario helps to naturally adjust the price to the correct amount. This means you must remain vigilant when looking to exploit them and be ready to act as soon as you detect the type of inconsistency you are looking for. If you are interested in trying forex arbitrage for yourself consider looking into an arbitrage calculator program. Free versions do exist but it is important to look at reviews and see what sort of results other traders have had with them before using one on an important trade.

Forex arbitrage opportunities are often hotly contested which means that if you do not get in early, you are better off not even bothering. Likewise, just because an inconsistency exists, does not mean that it is enough by itself to make the process worthwhile. Like most things, practice makes perfect and the only thing that can help you determine which arbitrage opportunities will yield profitable results.

Bitcoin trading

Bitcoins and other digital currencies have been shaking up the forex market since 2009. Bitcoins are an entirely digital currency whose current value is related to the total number of bitcoins in circulation. At the start of 2016, 1 bitcoin is worth roughly $420. When it comes to trading on forex using bitcoins you simply deposit your bitcoins into the digital wallet of a broker that accepts them (including Liteforex, eToro and AvaTrade among others). The funds then start off in the currency of your choice. Trading in bitcoins adds another layer to the forex equation as they tend to fluctuate independently of any other market. What this means is that using bitcoins to stimulate profits or to place profits somewhere more stable for a short period of time are both valid options.

Additional benefits include

- *Lots of leverage.* Leverage rates for bitcoins tend to be higher than average which is something that savvy traders can use to their advantage.

- *Lower transaction fees.* As bitcoins start out in a digital form that means they have less steps to cross when trading in Forex. This means less you have to pay out and higher profit margins in return. This goes for trading fees and deposit amounts as well.

Scalping

The next technique is known as scalping. Scalping is where the investor invests and sells of the currency within a matter of minutes. The basic idea is to capitalize on the fast changing difference in currency rates. This is mainly for those that want to finish off their daily trade fast and not keep thinking about it for the rest of the day. It is also for those that have a particular number in mind that they wish to make on a daily basis. You too should opt for this strategy if you want to realize a good profit on a daily basis and earn it within a short period of time.

Software

There are many types of software that are available, which will help you realize a big profit. This software is better known as artificial intelligence. You should look for the best one that will show you the way. However, a good and successful trader will never completely rely only on software. So, you have to do your research on the result that the software throws up. Once you are convinced, you can invest in it, if you are not convinced then don't invest in it at all.

These form the different expert approaches that you can take in the forex market to gain a profit from your investments.

Four Emotions Not to Have When Trading

Trading psychology and understandings its effects and consequences is important in forex because it helps in determining profits or losses. Keep in mind that brilliance and being book smart is not a guarantee that you would succeed in Forex. For example, the board of directors at LTCM includes Myron Scholes & Robert C. Merton, two Nobel Prize winners whose economic theories have contributed greatly to the modern world. However, their combined analytical skills would prove to be insufficient in saving LTCM from its untimely demise. Greed and euphoria took control over reason and leverage and subsequently increased the blow of false calculations.

LTCM suffered losses not because of they had no knowledge or expertise. Rather they had too much confidence, enthusiasm and a careless attitude to risk controls. Apart from good timing, traders must also know the different emotions that can spell doom or success when trading. Uncontrollable emotions do more damage than wrong analysis or the disregard of important information. A trader who masters not only forex knowledge or the psychology of it can walk away with profits so high.

Greed

It is only natural for forex investors to be spurred by money and driven by financial success. How else would they be able to compete in the forex market? Forex traders must be equipped with a strong drive for making money. This strong drive, in moderate amounts, is healthy, necessary and encouraged. However, these impulses are unhealthy when they influence trading decisions. Trading decisions are made with logic, patience, knowledge as well as instinct. With greed, your judgments can be clouded.

To ensure you don't become too greedy, always practice self-discipline. Go into the trading market with a strategy and remain focus on it. Decisions must be made on reason and analysis. A trader can achieve financial success in the forex market by learning from mistakes, refining trading methods and taking up disciplined and calculated applications.

Fear

Fear plays the opposite role of greed when it comes to trading decisions. A trader wrought with fear will act on impulse and not act on the basis of rational expectations and proper timing. A fearful trader will not be capable enough to make a distinction between losses as a result from wrong assumptions or losses due to miscalculations. To be a triumphant trader, one must practice some form of conservatism. Being conservative in our decision making process is always a sensible practice. You can be skeptical of things that you hear in the forex market but still be eager and able to act when your observations and calculations confirm a lucrative reward or a definite risk.

But a fearful trader is disbelieving of everything that anyone says, even his own analysis. Not knowing what steps to take, or how to remedy a situation or even who to trade with, a fearful trader might even disregard his own logic. The end result would be a panicky gambling with disastrous results.

To avoid fear, we need to practice our mind to comprehend that we alone are in control of our choices. As with avoiding greed, a clear trading plan will help us to follow logical solutions and keep a calm approach to trading. Traders must also not over leverage trading accounts.

Euphoria

Forex trading is no child's play and it is safe to assume that while huge profits are attainable in a short time in very select cases, some gains are really the work of long periods of study, reading, practice and strategies. For novice traders, small gains might cause a sense of euphoria as it might make the trader think that his knowledge and understanding of the forex market is enough, his analysis, techniques and strategies, flawless.

To prevent yourself from thinking this way, always remember that no analysis or strategy is flawless or fail-proof. Successful traders are always keeping an eye out and are skeptical of explanations, tips and techniques that come his way.

There is no sense of getting excited over a few moments of profits. Things change in the economy so what worked before might not work the next time. The key here is to always be diligent about your study of market conditions. The best way to avoid over excitement is by accepting that wins and losses do not determine the next trading session. A success or failure of the following session of trading is only determined by how competent we are as traders to use logic over emotions when it comes to market conditions.

Panic

When a trader panics, he sees nothing but losses in the market with no way of ending the session by turning the tables and making it a lucrative trade or a less disastrous one. In the forex market, when a trader loses a large sum of money, another trader is possibly earning large profits. This simple equation is enough at least to help traders to be much more practical in response to panic levels in the forex market. However, observation and experience has shown us anything, but.

There are many things that can cause traders in the forex market to panic such as market volatility, price fluctuations and so on. A frightful trader will definitely make different kinds of disastrous errors from closing positions too early to performing away from his logical analysis and be driven by illusions and emotions. All in all, the panicky trader can barely contain his demeanor, thus intensifying damage.

When trading in the forex market, traders must learn to not let their emotions influence their trading decisions. Minimizing the role of emotions is the key to understand how to manage crisis.

Leverage is always the control of the forex account owner therefore she can set it at any value, but bearing in mind the consequences. While leverage amplifies the gains or losses of a trade, it also amplifies the emotional response of trading as well. Eventually, emotional pressures may prove to be the most dangerous and negative impact of leverage. To deal with emotional problems is to look at things at a practical and logical approach. The easiest way to do that is to learn, study and understand market behavior.

Trading Tips from the Experts

'Forex is too risky!'

'Don't rely on instincts. Only technical analysis works'

'You can only predict short-term markets'

'You can only predict long-term markets'

'Forex is difficult'

'Forex is easy'

So what do all these statements have in common? Well, they are all beliefs that traders have about the market and all these statements shape the forex trading psychology.

Beliefs... can be painful. And should you listen to them?

Well, while some beliefs are the result of traumatic experiences, they are not necessarily bad. Beliefs serve a purpose in our lives whether in trading or non-trading aspects. While they aren't bad, they aren't entirely useful to listen to when it comes to the forex market.

There are no defined zones in the trading marketplace. You have no teacher, no parent, no boss and no rules to control what you do. You have the choice to trade in whichever way you like. So whatever beliefs you have, these are your beliefs.

Say for example if you read a piece of news or a price action on a chart. Your belief that it may or may not influence market conditions and this belief is the reason you took action. From this point of decision making, you have traced a path back to a belief (or a series of beliefs) that caused you to take that action.

Your beliefs can be on many things such as your choice to trade in a specific currency pair or even your choice of strategy. Your belief is the one guiding you to make these decisions. Being aware of your belief is a powerful thing and a catalyst for change.

Beliefs are at the most basic level, evolutionary.

Some beliefs are part of our DNA whereas some are a product of the environment we live in. Some beliefs are indoctrinated in us. For the most part of our lives, we absorb these beliefs and never question them but along the way, some of these beliefs are challenged. Think about the belief that deodorant could cause breast cancer. Is it true? It is not true? Where did this belief stem from?

So is belief useful to us traders? Van K. Tharp once said that 'We Trade our Beliefs about the Market'. There are indeed many different approaches as there are many different traders and each of them belief different things. But as traders or even people in general, we only see what we want to see.

As traders, we decide what we want to belief in and decide which of these beliefs can be instrumental in helping us gain success in the Foreign Exchange market.

The Beliefs of Top Traders

George Soros- His name is synonymous with the trading world. Soros rose to fame when he became the trader who broke the Bank of England, netting him a profit of $1 billion after short selling $10 billion in GBP. Soros, who came up with the theory of reflexivity believes that participants in the market itself directly influence market fundamentals. Their sometimes rational and sometimes irrational behavior is the one that leads to booms and busts that open up investment opportunities.

Geraldine Weiss- She was one of the first women in the foreign exchange world. She learned about investments from reading books and listening to her parent's conversations and then later on in college. Weiss belief is to combine blue-chip investment style with a value approach and she uses dividend yields as a guide to value. Her value-based dividend oriented stock picking strategy proved to be successful even in poor markets.

Andrew Krieger- He acquired a reputation as a successful trader when he joined Banker's Trust in 1986. The company then rewarded him by increasing his capital limit to $700 million which put Krieger in a perfect position to profit from the Black Monday October 19, 1987 crash. He believed that the New Zealand dollar was vulnerable to short selling and applied a startling leverage of 400:1, thus acquiring him a position bigger than the New Zealand money supply. The result of this netted him $300 million in profits for Banker's Trust.

Bruce Kovner- His first trade was at 32 years old in 1977. He borrowed from his personal credit card to purchase soybean futures contract which netted him a profit of $20,000. When he joined Commodities Corporation as a trader, Kovner became a successful trader booking millions in profits. Kovner believed that having an exceptional mind in Math and science was fundamental to trading successfully, without worrying about finance credentials.

Muriel Sibert- She obtained an entry-level research position, despite not having a college degree, in finance and eventually became partner. She went on to open the brokerage firm named Muriel Sibert & Co in 1967 but could not register her firm due to gender discrimination. Muriel persevered and eventually her firm became the first woman-owned member of the NYSE. Muriel believed in bringing in new ideas and eventually turned her company into a discount brokerage, which was a new model at that time.

Joseph Siegel- A successful trader and investor, Seigel said that traders can really benefit on the market if they were confident of themselves. Confidence comes from the belief that your success is from your hard work and disciplined trading. Starting slow and working your way up is essential especially for novice traders. He also said to never be jealous of other traders. Learning to belief in yourself and understanding yourself gives you an edge over other traders.

Chapter 6: Mistakes to Avoid in the forex Market

The forex market is a vast place and there are hundreds of transactions that take place in a single day. You have to understand that it is easy to slip up in the market and so; you have to exercise a little precaution. We looked at the different winning strategies that you have to employ in the forex market and in this chapter; we will look at the different mistakes that you have to avoid.

Fancy indicators

Many new investors make the mistake of thinking that they need invest in fancy tools and buy software that will give them an advantage in the stock market. This is not true. There is no need for any of these fancy tools and indicators if you wish to make it big in the forex market. It is enough if you understand to read a price chart properly. Just because a certain trader has access to these does not mean he or she will be able to profit greatly. It all depends on your assessment of the situation and what you plan to do with your currency pairs.

Not understanding risk

One of the biggest mistakes that most new traders make in the forex market is not understand the risk that it poses. The forex market is a vast place where there is a lot of scope for risk. You have to make use of a stop loss if you are trading on a daily basis. The stop loss refers to a limit that you place on the currency to protect you from a loss. Say for example you set a stop loss of $2 on your investment with the yuan. This means that if the price does drop by $2 then you will automatically be removed from the trade. Now, just by placing a wider margin like say $10, you will not be risking more or by placing a lesser margin like $1, you will not be risking less. You have to choose the stop loss margin based on how low the price might actually fall. Experience will teach you to pick the right stop loss.

Not have a plan

You will end up undergoing a big loss if you do not have a proper plan to work with. There is no point in trying to go about the trading without a proper plan. There are those that think they can go about investing in the market without a plan and still earn riches just because that was the case when they started out. But your beginners luck will not work for you for a long time. It will run out and so will your finances. So, you have to come up with a good plan to invest in the market. The plan can include setting attainable goals and pursuing them. These plans are what will help the trader grow and make the right investment choices.

Gambling

There are many people that make the mistake of gambling instead of investing. Some people will seek a certain thrill out of the investments and try to gamble with currencies that are not good bets. They will seek a certain thrill out being on the edge and will not be disappointed if they lose the money. This can be a dangerous thing and the person will fall into a vicious cycle. You have to showcase responsibility while investing in the market. Don't make the mistake of taking it lightly. You have to be as serious as possible if you wish to make the most of your forex investments.

Investing emotionally

This is one of those mistakes that people make without realizing it. They will get emotionally attached to a currency pair and invest only in it. The currency might be doing badly which will cause you to lose money. So, don't get attached to any of the currencies. You have to treat them as tools used to profit from. If at any time they are causing you a loss then you should immediately stop investing in it. If it is getting a bit too clouded for you then you should take a step back and assess the situation.

Not being patient

Some people don't have patience whatsoever. They will remain fidgety and want to keep doing one thing or the other. Such people will end up losing a lot of money in the forex market. It is understood that the forex market is a bit stable but if you remain too worried and try to dispose off your currencies all at once even before it reaches its best value then you will end up losing money. You have to make an investment and remain patient. Once the currency reaches the ideal price you can dispose it off.

Waiting too long

Some traders will not know when to stop and hold on to their currencies for a very long time. That is completely wrong as the currency value will start falling and you will lose out on your profits. When the time looks right you have to sell your currencies. You have to make use of the pattern predictions, as that is what will help you understand the best time when you can dispose of the currencies.

These form the different mistakes that you have to avoid in the forex market.

The Power of Belief

Different traders have different beliefs about the market and all these statements shape the forex trading psychology.

Beliefs... can be painful. And should you listen to them?

Well, while some beliefs are the result of traumatic experiences, they are not necessarily bad. Beliefs serve a purpose in our lives whether in trading or non-trading aspects. While they aren't bad, they aren't entirely useful to listen to when it comes to the forex market.

Say for example if you read a piece of news or a price action on a chart. Your belief that it may or may not influence market conditions and this belief is the reason you took action. From this point of decision making, you have traced a path back to a belief (or a series of beliefs) that caused you to take that action.

Your beliefs can be on many things such as your choice to trade in a specific currency pair or even your choice of strategy. Your belief is the one guiding you to make these decisions. Being aware of your belief is a powerful thing and a catalyst for change.

Beliefs are at the most basic level, evolutionary.

Some beliefs are part of our DNA whereas some are a product of the environment we live in. Some beliefs are indoctrinated in us. For the most part of our lives, we absorb these beliefs and never question them but along the way, some of these beliefs are challenged. Think about the belief that deodorant could cause breast cancer. Is it true? It is not true? Where did this belief stem from?

So is belief useful to us traders? Van K. Tharp once said that 'We Trade our Beliefs about the Market'. There are indeed many different approaches as there are many different traders and each of them belief different things. But as traders or even people in general, we only see what we want to see.

As traders, we decide what we want to belief in and decide which of these beliefs can be instrumental in helping us gain success in the Foreign Exchange market.

Chapter 7: Essential Do's and Don'ts of forex

In this chapter, we will look at the different dos and don'ts of forex trading that you have to understand in order to conduct smooth sailing trade.

Dos

Understand the potential

The very first thing is to understand the true potential of the forex market. You have to take in the sheer size of it and account for the millions of traders that will engage in trade on a daily basis. You should understand that the forex market is capable of leaving you with a huge profit and give you the chance to control hundreds of thousands of dollars just with a small investment. Being prepared for all this is the key to your success in the forex market.

Time frame

You have to set a reasonable time frame for your forex investments to grow in value. Like any business or stock market investment, you have to consider a time period that is at least a month to 5 years old. You have to invest a little in all types of currencies that will showcase their true potential over differing periods of time. So, you have to invest a little in those that will mature in 5 years, some in 1 year, some in 6 months, some in a month, some within a week etc. Having a diverse investment plan will only work to your benefit.

Assess risks

You have to assess your risks in the currency market. There are many risks that can prevail and you have to be well acquainted with each. Some of the most prominent risks including shorting a profitable currency is investing in one that is moving at a sluggish pace. You have to bear these in mind when you enter into the forex market. Do your best to place your risks ahead of your gains just to be prepared for the worst. Once you eliminate that fear, you will be able to trade better in the market.

Risk capital

You have to make use of risk capital if you wish to invest freely in the forex market. Risk capital refers to money that you are willing to risk in the market and will not be worried even if you lose the money in a bad trade. The money has to be your personal money and not any borrowed money. If you don't have enough resources as yet to invest in the market then wait for some time to earn it and only then start your forex trade.

Do Research

When getting into Forex, you must not only have a plan, you should already do some research of current trends, market conditions as well as the different commodities and stocks available to trade in. Traders must also know that the pillars of successful forex trading are a combination of knowledge and understanding of the Foreign Exchange Trade and its life-cycle. Some information on the present monetary market will come in handy and a good reading on the dynamics and basics of forex is a must.

Keep in mind gain & loss ratio

Knowing that there will always be losses as there will be gains will help a trader execute logical decisions when trading. If you are a new trader, always begin trading when the market is progressively growing up or going down. The ratio of gains and loss will also help him or her to keep on track with their trading plan.

Have a winning mindset

"Wherever you are, make sure you're there". Dan Sullivan, Strategic Coach Founder

We said this before- think of the forex market like a battlefield and any soldier going into the battlefield needs preparation and the right attitude. So set yourself up with the right, winning mindset because you will then subconsciously re-program your brain to profit.

Statistically, trading is a difficult proposition with a failure rate of 90 percent. It is important to keep this in mind when you hit what is a seemingly endless string of bad trades. The odds are always against you which is why you should do your best to make every single trade count. You never know when you will get another win so it is a good idea to treat this one as delicately as possible.

Set a daily trade limit and stick to it

This can be a difficult habit to get into, especially for new traders but it is essential for a number of reasons. First, it will help you to keep going even if your first few trades of the day did not turn out well. Forex trading is a speculative business; no one can be right all of the time. Your goal should be to average more good trades then bad ones each day, that's all. This will also help to ensure that you do not make finicky trades. Your goal should always be to wait until a trade is presenting clear signals before you pounce on it. Without setting a limit to the trades you will make in a day you will mostly likely find it more difficult to wait until the optimum moment to make the trade. Force yourself to make every trade count, set a daily limit.

Master one currency

When it comes to technical trading, it is important to start by learning everything there is to know about a single currency and then expanding your knowledge from there. This can be a difficult idea for new traders to understand as currency is traded in pairs. Regardless, it is important to first learn all of the unique things about one currency before you move on to another. Starting with a solid foundation in a single currency will allow you to fall back on what you do know when you come across an area with which you are less familiar.

Learn from successful traders

Successful traders, like some of the successful people in the world have a few common traits. They have perseverance, drive, determination, patience and a positive approach. While everyone throws the towel away, they get even more determined. They go back with a need to return much stronger.

They keep notes, they learn from their mistakes, they apply their lessons and they also thrive on independence. Trading not only needs creativity and intelligent solutions, it also needs stamina and confidence. Successful traders never doubt their worth.

Leo Malamed, the pioneer in the concept of foreign currency futures and the person behind the creation of the International Monetary Market points out that to be a successful trader is to realize the capacity to take a loss. No risk taker is going to be right every time. Malamed points out that a trader needs two elements- one, the readiness to take a risk and two, the capability to admit that you are wrong. He also stresses that you cannot let your emotions get in the way because this will carry to your upcoming trade and cause another loss.

Perform weekend analysis

At the end of every trade week, when markets are closed look at your weekly charts to study patterns or read up business news that may affect your trade. By doing this every weekend, this is where your best plans would be hatched. When you have your plan, stick to it because although the market does not reach your point of entry, never fret. Learn to sit on your hands. Patience is virtue and good things come to those who wait. When you do miss a trade, wait for the next one and do better.

Keep a record

Keeping a journal of your trading patterns is the best tool a trader can give to himself. In your records, list all the reasons for your trade and include fundamentals that may affect you from your decisions. On your chart, mark the entry and exit points and add in any relevant comments and feedback. Keep this information filed so you can always refer to it anytime. In your records, also note down your emotional reactions when you made a decision. Were you in panic? Greedy? Anxious? When you objectify your trades, you will naturally develop mental control and discipline.

Don'ts

Choose wrong currencies

Some people end up choosing the wrong currencies to trade in. this means that they will pick two currencies that don't have a wide gap between them or go to the extremes and pick the ones that have the widest gap. The idea is to find the middle path and pick two that will help you realize a sizeable profit. You have to rely on some recommendations from your broker or a currency expert. There are many websites that will help you pick the best.

Believing emails

Don't make the mistake of believing whatever you read in the emails. This means that you should not trust just about any information that you might get. You have to especially beware of emails that might come from so-called market experts. These emails will be mass generated and will not be tailored for you. You have to do your own research before falling prey to any of these emails.

Message boards

Do not fall prey to message board scams. These message boards are a prominent feature on most trading websites. There will be pumpers and bashers present on it who will try to control the forex market. The pumpers will force people to buy a currency just to increase its value and the bashers will bad mouth it to cause a drop in its value. You have to beware of both and not fall into any of the traps that these boards set up. You have to only rely on your own research if you wish to make profits.

Choose wrong broker

You will be making a big mistake by choosing the wrong broker for yourself. It is essential that you choose one that is not only well reputed but also has enough experience in the field of Forex. You have to look at his testimonials and then decide for yourself. If you and your broker are not on the same page and end up having tiffs regularly then you should change your broker at the earliest. Ask your trading company to assign you the best one in their firm.

Copy strategies

You have to remember that there is no one size fits all in the forex market. You have to choose a different approach to investing in forex depending on the market situation. You have to tailor make a plan for yourself and follow through with it. If you think you can copy someone else's strategy just because they were able to turn in the riches then you will be making a big mistake. Sit down and come up with an individual winning strategy for yourself and pursue it. Only then will you be able to get the best out of your forex investments.

These form the different dos and don'ts of forex trade that you have to bear in mind while investing in the market.

Trade without a plan

"Obstacles are those frightful things you see when you take your eyes off your goal". Henry Ford

Like we mentioned before, having a plan, a system and a methodology will help you stir your ship in the trading market sea. Forex involves a plan if you want to accomplish the most efficient results. No plan, no profit to put it simply. With a well established forex trading plan, you will be prepared to face numerous trading scenarios and no matter what scenario comes your way, your plan will help you come through the toughest scenarios.

A plan also helps you keep your goals aligned to your instruments and it always helps you stay focused. A plan also helps you track your progress efficiently especially when you have set yourself milestones to achieve.

Your plans will also help you make the right decisions and not act on impulse. You can take immediate actions that can remedy a loss by lessening the loss or by breaking even. Most importantly, a plan helps you stick to your methodology and it minimizes emotional influences in your decision making.

Let emotions get in the way of logical judgment

We've talked about this one in the previous chapter. The biggest mistake a trader can make is basing a decision or acting based on their emotions involving the state of a trade.

Whether you win or lose- there is always a lesson learned. Many experienced traders often say that to become a good trader, you must experience loss otherwise you will not know what you did wrong and you will be too confident in your methodology to review it again or test it. Losses also encourage a trader to trade even more so she can gain back what she lost. A chain of losses may bring dissatisfaction and bad decisions whereas a string of wins may lead to overconfidence.

Also, when a trader gets too emotionally involved, he or she may lose patience. Patience is a virtue and this statement cannot be underestimated especially in the forex market. Patience to test and patience to check, patience to even wait for the right timing to trade.

Also, logic must prevail over emotions when trading. Using logic will help in making the best decisions for your trade thus generating better results and lessening the risk of a loss. One must be more logical than emotional when trading in Forex. This ultimately leads to a trader making the best decisions in the trade therefore generating better trades and lesser risk of loss.

Chairman of Chicago Mercantile Exchange, John Sandner says that traders have to be constantly focused and pay attention to what they are doing and what their program is.

Once you are focused, discipline will follow. A good way to practice focus and discipline is to surround yourself with positive traders because gradually, you will follow their behavior model.

Gamble

When you walk into the trading market, never think that forex is the equivalent of gambling. While they are both similar with risks and returns, forex trading requires logical decisions to be made, it requires a plan, it requires calculated moves and it also requires a system and methodology. You need all these in forex trading because when a situation does follow according to your plan, you can counter this by making constructive measures to remedy the situation.

While all these tips and tricks are something to learn and follow, in the midst of trading, it can be quite tricky to follow. However, it is always good to practice these guidelines every time you trade, and then it'll be second nature to you.

Straddle the line

One of the most common mistakes many people make when they first begin trading regularly is they pay a brokerage to trade for them while also trying to do what they can to uncover and follow leads and find good trades on their own. This will only create a gulf between you and your brokerage and cause you nothing but headaches as a result. If you made the decision to let a brokerage handle your trades, then let them do what you pay them for. If you enjoy making your own moves based on your own research however, then cut the cord and make your own trades all of the time. A mixed approach will only find you holding information that you can't act on and a feeling of anger if an idea you had but couldn't implement actually bears fruit.

Have some but not all of the information you need

Many new traders will take the time to do research, but then stick the landing when it comes to execution or understanding the entirety of an issue. A little information is a dangerous thing and this goes double when it comes to forex trading. As you know, forex trading happens in pairs, this means that every time you set out to research a trade you need to be completely sure about both sides of the equation. Having a hunch about one currency, even if you are right, is only half of the battle. This is also why it is important to never commit to any trades during off hours as this is a time period during which you as an individual will not profit. Hedge funds, option traders and banks have additional options during these periods that you cannot hope to match as an individual. This means you can easily find yourself working without outdated information without even realizing it.

Likewise, it is important to follow up on the trends of any currency you are thinking about purchasing to ensure that the information you have is an accurate reflection of reality. Without doing the proper research you could easily find yourself picking up a currency at what seems like a great deal only to watch the bottom continue to fall out of the currency after you purchased it. You want to pick up currency on the cheap. You don't want to do so when it is already in the midst of a freefall with no end in sight. This will also allow you to find better deals as you will be more aware when something really has bottomed out and has no choice but to climb again.

Exit trades improperly

Exiting trades in the proper fashion is just as important as making them at the correct time. If you find yourself in a situation where a trade is not performing as expected there are a number of ways, you can extricate yourself from it besides a simple stop order. For example, what is known a trailing stop can be placed by setting the percentage amount you are willing to let the currency change from the market price as it exists now. This type of stop allows you to prevent losses while at the same time providing you with the ability to generate gains as long as the market is looking up.

A trailing stop is more effective than a fixed stop as it is inherently more flexible and able to respond to a wider variety of variables. The difference between your stop point and the current price is also automatically tracked which means you don't have to be as hands on as you do with a fixed stop. It also allows you to mitigate losses because you can set the stop to trigger if the price ever falls by a set amount in a single day.

An easy way to ensure that you are always on track to maximize your profits is to combine both the trailing stop and the traditional stop together. To do this you must first determine your level of risk tolerance and set a fixed stop based on that information. From there you set a trailing stop at a point lower than the fixed stop point.

Assuming the trade moves in your favor than the initial stop loss will be made obsolete at which point you can set a new one and let the process repeat itself.

Think too much

While it is a good idea to do as much research as possible when deciding on a pair to trade, it is equally important to ensure that you don't over think what could be an otherwise fairly straightforward trade. Start by setting a profit target floor and never undertaking any trade that falls beneath it. In addition, following trends will result in higher profits than looking for bargains so stick to trading during the highest periods of traffic, more volume means more results.

In addition to overanalyzing, it is important to have the right amount of both confidence and courage. When you have taken the time to do the research and calculate the odds, you need to have the confidence to believe in yourself and follow through. It is important to not be overconfident however; doing so will let the reality of a situation get lost behind a veil of unwarranted confidence. Don't mistake pride for confidence. If a trade goes south, know enough to walk away.

Likewise, letting a loss ride shouldn't be mistaken for courage either. Know enough to understand that sometimes a trade will turn on you for a completely unexpected reason and you have to get out while the getting is good. Betting on a trade that has visibly turned will only lead to greater losses. Suck it up and try again tomorrow.

Finally, it is important to always focus on the matter at hand rather than dreaming about ideal trades or fantasy scenarios. Forex trading is all about relying on hard facts, there is no room for anything else if you want to be successful. Making the correct trades day in and day out should require all of your attention, if you divide part of your time dreaming about trades you wished you made will only make the trades you do make less effective overall.

Confuse quantity with quality

The average human mind can only provide its full attention to a task in 90 minute increments, anything more than that quickly reaches a point when the amount of effort put into achieving progress rapidly outpaces the results. forex trading takes complete focus in order to be effective, don't hurt your daily trade averages, take frequent breaks and never trade for more than 3 hours a day, say a 90-minute period in the morning and again in the mid-afternoon. That doesn't mean you shouldn't keep tabs on the news and whatnot during the off time, but it does mean that you shouldn't waste your day staring at numbers that won't move for hours at a time. Do yourself a favor and let the market do its job, you will be glad you did.

This adage works for the type of trades you make as well as time you spend making them. It is easy to make several low-risk trades during the day and as a result only see a small dividend or loss at the end of the day. You will find that you can be much more productive once you learn how to pull the trigger on trades that have bigger potential losses but also vastly superior gains.

Chapter 8: FAQs on forex Trading

Finally, we will take a look at some frequently asked questions on this topic that will help you increase your knowledge on the subject matter.

Should I be a professional investor to trade in Forex?

No. You do not have to be a bona fide investor to start trading in the forex market. It will no doubt help a great deal if you are already aware of the different ways in which the stock market operates and understand the principles but they are not a necessity. You can easily understand start trading in the forex market if you have sufficient knowledge about it. This book will push you in the right direction and help you get started. From there onwards, the markets will guide you.

What is a good amount to start with?

There is no such thing as a good amount. How much you want to invest in the market is completely your choice. It can be $100 or $1000. It can be more than that as well. You have to pick an amount that is good enough to help you get started in the forex market and invest in lucrative currencies. Some companies might ask you to deposit a minimum amount with them, which you have to maintain if you wish to trade with them. If it lapses below the minimum amount then you might be charged a fine for it.

Does experience count?

Yes. Experience will work wonders in the forex market. While starting out, you might not know how to go about it the right way or have the patience for it. But after you undergo a few losses owing to your mistakes, you will turn wiser. You should not be too harsh on yourself and have to maintain your calm composure. If at any time you feel like it is a bit too overwhelming, then you have to take a short break and then return to the trade once again. You have to remain confident and develop a never give up attitude.

Is a broker a must?

No. Hiring a broker is completely your choice. You can easily trade in forex without the help of a broker. You have to open an online account and buy and sell the currencies. The broker is mainly employed by those that are not aware of the functioning of the forex market or those that do not have the time for it. If you have both of these then you can avoid hiring a broker, as he will only bring about an extra expense. Even if you do wish to hire a broker then pick a part time one as opposed to a full time broker. But beware, some brokers will not be up to the mark and might end up causing you loses. You have to test out the broker to see if he is a good choice.

Can I hold and earn?

Yes. You don't have to dispose off your currencies just because you are in a hurry to make money. The value of any investment grows over time and so will your foreign currency investments. You have to remain patient and hold on to your currencies until such time as it grows in value. This can range between a few weeks to years. Once the currency prices reach the highest point, you can dispose them off and come into profit.

Can I accumulate?

Yes. You can accumulate the currencies. If a certain currency has dipped in value then you can buy more of it to help increase the average. This means that instead of panicking, you have to buy more in order to realize a profit from it. Some impatient traders will be in a hurry to dispose it off and also do it to try and save themselves from a loss. That is not the approach you should be taking if you wish to profit from the forex markets.

Can I transfer the currencies?

Yes. You can transfer the currencies that you are holding to another person. You will have the choice of doing so through your trading account. You have to speak with the company and tell them to whom you wish to transfer the currency. The company might charge a small fee for the transaction but it will only be a one-time thing. The person receiving the money might have to acknowledge the receipt of the currencies.

Can I pump in profits?

Yes. What you do with your profits is up to you. You can use it to fund your future forex investments or also simply keep it as a reward for your trading. Remember that you must not invest more than 8 to 10% of your money in any one of the currencies. You will end up making a mistake if you do so as you will be worried about all your money going downhill.

Is the news the only source for information?

No. You can also sign up for company newsletters that will keep you updated about the different trends in the forex market. You can also consult with your broker to understand the trends. There are many things apart from relying on the news that you can do to gather information on the forex markets.

Can I stop anytime?

Yes, starting and stopping is entirely up to you. If you think you have profited enough from the forex market then you can stop with it. There is no rule or compulsion for you to carry on with it for long. But if you are doing well then there is no point in stopping with it. However, if you are unable to tap into the potential of the forex markets then it is best that you not invest in it any further and only return after you have devised a good come back plan.

What guarantees do I have?

Unlike options, futures or stocks, forex trading is not limited to a regulated exchange. This means there is no ruling body that is in charge of setting up clearing houses of insuring that trades are made in good faith. Trades are made between parties with the help of credit agreements and little else. It may be helpful to think of forex trades as being sealed with a handshake while all other trades are made with formal contracts. While this may seem prone to error in theory, in practice there is a fair amount of self-regulation which occurs because every trader must be able to cooperate with any other to trade effectively. As such, traders which cannot be trusted cannot expect to be traders for long.

How do brokers make money?

Once again, this is a point where the forex market differs from its peers in that forex brokerages actually work as dealers instead of in a traditional broker capacity. As dealers, they assume a greater level of risk but do not make their money by charging a commission on trades. Instead, they use something called the bid-ask spread to ensure they are compensated for their efforts. This can be thought of as the difference in the amount a currency is worth versus how much the brokerage found someone willing to pay. This way you get the standard asking price at the current moment and the brokerage gets anything above that.

What exactly am I buying and selling?

The short answer to this question is nothing, though it is actually more complicated than that. The forex market is one that is exclusively speculative in nature and the currency being discussed is little more than numbers that correspond to one another across a myriad of computer databases. The market exists primarily so that major corporations can trade currencies more easily while moving across various continents so they can do things like conduct payroll and pay local vendors. The brokerage and individual speculative markets that have sprung up as a result are only a side effect despite comprising a majority of the daily exchange market.

These form the different FAQs on the topic and we hope you found it informative.

Key Highlights

It is understood that there are many ways in which you can trade in the stock market but one of the most preferred and best ways to pick is the forex market. You have to understand what forex stands for and how you can use it to your advantage.

The forex market refers to foreign exchange. As you know, each and every country has its own currency. These currencies will not all be valued at the same rate and will have different rates assigned to them. One country's currency will trail another country's. You, as a forex investor will have to identify the two countries whose currencies will help you realize a profit. So say you bought 200 pound sterling by exchanging 300 dollars and then used the pounds to buy 1000 yuan. Here, you have managed to make a big profit from the transaction and that forms the very basis of Forex.

But it will not always be as easy. The prices are extremely volatile and you have to especially be careful when you are investing large sums of money. The very first thing to do is come up with a trading plan to follow. The plan should be such that it allows you to make all the best decisions in the forex market. You cannot take it for granted and must stick with the plan for as long as you wish to remain with profits.

You have to get started with forex trading by doing a few essential things. This includes buying a laptop, getting an internet connection, opening an account, downloading the software, hiring a broker increasing your knowledge on the subject etc. All of these will push you in the right direction and get you started with forex trading.

We looked at the different places that help with your forex investments. You can choose any of them and start trading at the earliest.

There are three main types of calculations and indices that you have to prepare if you wish to invest in the forex market. The first type is known as the fundamental analysis and deals with understanding the different economic and political factors that might affect the value of the currency. The technical analysis helps in predicting the values that the currencies might take on based on their past trends. You have to try and calculate everything correctly to profit from your forex investments. If you don't know how to do it then you can take the help of software that will calculate for you.

We looked at the different winning strategies that you have to adopt in order to make it big in the forex market. You have to make smart choices if you wish to make a big profit. These strategies are implemented by some of the most successful forex traders in the world. Of course experience counts when it comes to making profits but you have to try your best to do the right thing from the very beginning and lay down a strong foundation for your forex trade.

The dos and don'ts were provided for your reference and are meant to strengthen your tactics. You have to treat them as guidelines to follow in order to remain with profits. You can modify them and come up with your own list of dos and don'ts if you wish to increase your profit margins. You have to also create a gettable goal list. It is like a goal setting process where you set out things to achieve. Once you achieve them, you have to check them off the list and move to the next goal.

We looked at the different mistakes that you must avoid in the forex market. They are some of the most common mistakes that are committed and you have to steer clear of them if you wish to remain in profit. Some people consider forex investments, as gambling options but that is not the right way to go about it and you should treat as a means to increase your money's worth.

As a final word of advice, you have to remain patient with the forex market and make smart choices if you wish to make the most of your investments.

Conclusion

I thank you once again for choosing this book and hope you had a good time reading it.

The main aim of this book was to share with you the basic steps and strategies of forex trading.

I hope you have understood the different aspects of forex trading and will be able to carry it out easily.

If at any time you have a doubt about the trade then you can always refer back to this book and have your doubts cleared.

I wish you luck with your foreign exchange endeavors.

All the best!

Special Invitation!

If you liked what you read and would like to read high quality books, get free bonuses, and get notified first of **FREE EBOOKS,** then join the official Xcension Publishing Company Book Club! Membership is free, but space is limited!

Join the Book Club by visiting the link below:

http://www.xcensionpublishing.com/book-club